Clean Jokes for kids!

Sola Printing

HOW DOES A SCIENTIST FRESHEN HER BREATH?

WITH EXPERI-MINTS.

TWO PICKLES FELL OUT OF A JAR ONTO THE FLOOR. WHAT DID ONE SAY TO THE OTHER?

DILL WITH IT.

WHAT DO YOU CALL A BOOMERANG THAT WON'T COME BACK?

A STICK.

WHAT DOES A CLOUD WEAR UNDER HIS RAINCOAT?

THUNDERWEAR.

WHAT TIME IS IT WHEN THE CLOCK STRIKES 13?

TIME TO GET A NEW CLOCK.

HOW DOES A CUCUMBER BECOME A PICKLE?

IT GOES THROUGH A JARRING EXPERIENCE.

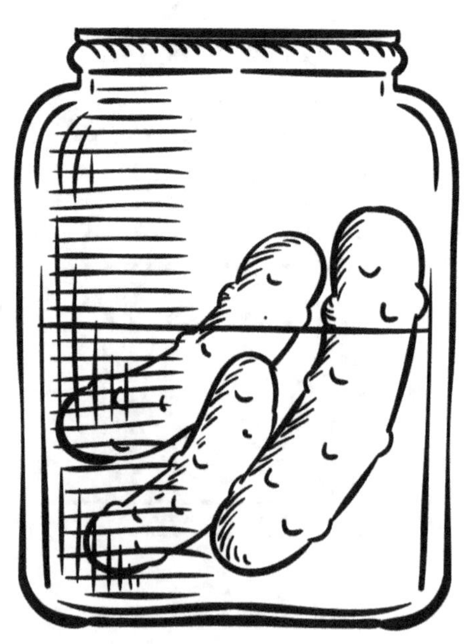

WHAT DID ONE TOILET SAY TO THE OTHER?

YOU LOOK A BIT FLUSHED.

WHAT DO YOU THINK OF THAT NEW DINER ON THE MOON?

FOOD WAS GOOD, BUT THERE REALLY WASN'T MUCH ATMOSPHERE.

WHAT MUSICAL INSTRUMENT IS FOUND IN THE BATHROOM?

A TUBA TOOTHPASTE.

HOW DO YOU GET A SQUIRREL TO LIKE YOU?

ACT LIKE A NUT.

WHAT DO YOU CALL TWO BIRDS IN LOVE?

TWEETHEARTS

HOW ARE FALSE TEETH LIKE STARS?

THEY COME OUT AT NIGHT.

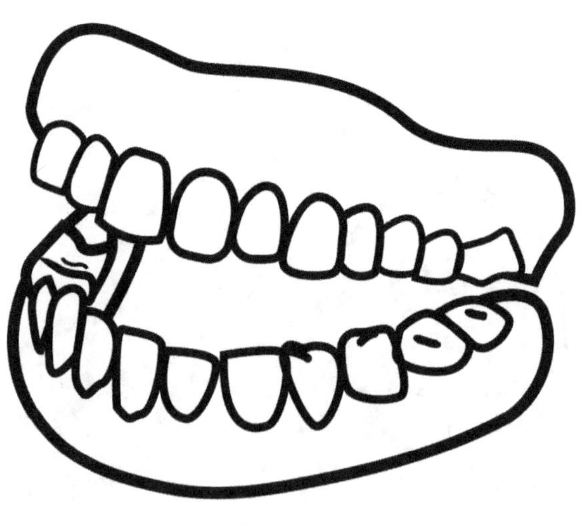

WHAT BUILDING IN YOUR TOWN HAS THE MOST STORIES?

THE PUBLIC LIBRARY.

WHAT'S WORSE THAN FINDING A WORM IN YOUR APPLE?

FINDING HALF A WORM.

WHAT IS A COMPUTER'S FAVORITE SNACK?

COMPUTER CHIPS.

WHAT DID ONE VOLCANO SAY TO THE OTHER?

I LAVA YOU.

HOW DO WE KNOW THAT THE OCEAN IS FRIENDLY?

IT WAVES.

WHAT IS A TORNADO'S FAVORITE GAME TO PLAY?

TWISTER.

HOW DOES THE MOON CUT HIS HAIR?

ECLIPSE IT.

HOW DO YOU TALK TO A GIANT?

USE BIG WORDS.

WHAT FALLS IN WINTER BUT NEVER GETS HURT?

SNOW.

WHAT DID THE DALMATIAN SAY AFTER LUNCH?

THAT HIT THE SPOT.

WHY DID THE COOKIE GO TO THE HOSPITAL?

BECAUSE HE FELT CRUMMY.

WHY WAS THE BABY STRAWBERRY CRYING?

BECAUSE HER MOM AND DAD WERE IN A JAM.

WHAT DID THE LITTLE CORN SAY TO THE MAMA CORN?

WHERE IS POP CORN?

WHAT DID THE LIMESTONE SAY TO THE GEOLOGIST?

DON'T TAKE ME FOR GRANITE.

WHY DOES A SEAGULL FLY OVER THE SEA?

BECAUSE IF IT FLEW OVER THE BAY, IT WOULD BE A BAYGULL.

WHAT KIND OF WATER CAN'T FREEZE?

HOT WATER.

WHAT KIND OF TREE FITS IN YOUR HAND?

A PALM TREE.

WHAT DO YOU CALL A DINOSAUR THAT IS SLEEPING?

A DINO-SNORE.

WHAT IS FAST, LOUD AND CRUNCHY?

A ROCKET CHIP.

WHY DID THE TEDDY BEAR SAY NO TO DESSERT?

BECAUSE SHE WAS STUFFED.

WHAT DID THE LEFT EYE SAY TO THE RIGHT EYE?

BETWEEN US, SOMETHING SMELLS.

WHAT DID ONE PLATE SAY TO THE OTHER PLATE?

DINNER IS ON ME.

WHAT DO YOU SAY TO A RABBIT ON ITS BIRTHDAY?

HOPPY BIRTHDAY.

WHY DID THE STUDENT EAT HIS HOMEWORK?

BECAUSE THE TEACHER TOLD HIM IT WAS A PIECE OF CAKE.

WHAT'S THE ONE THING YOU WILL GET EVERY YEAR ON YOUR BIRTHDAY, GUARANTEED?

A YEAR OLDER.

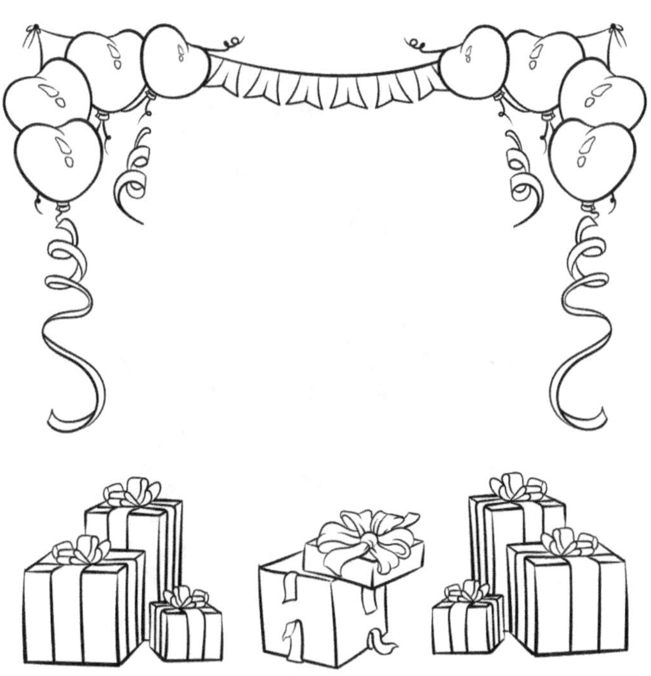

WHY DIDN'T THE QUARTER ROLL DOWN THE HILL WITH THE NICKEL?

BECAUSE IT HAD MORE CENTS.

WHY IS THE OBTUSE TRIANGLE ALWAYS SO FRUSTRATED?

BECAUSE IT'S NEVER RIGHT.

WHY WAS THE EQUAL SIGN SO HUMBLE?

BECAUSE HE WASN'T GREATER THAN OR LESS THAN ANYONE ELSE.

WHY WAS THE MATH BOOK SAD?

BECAUSE IT HAD TOO MANY PROBLEMS.

WHY COULDN'T THE PONY SING A LULLABY?

SHE WAS A LITTLE HORSE.

WHAT DID THE BANANA SAY TO THE DOG?

BANANAS CAN'T TALK.

HOW DO YOU FIT MORE PIGS ON A FARM?

BUILD A STY-SCRAPER.

WHAT DID THE FARMER CALL THE COW THAT HAD NO MILK?

AN UDDER FAILURE.

WHAT DO YOU GET FROM A PAMPERED COW?

SPOILED MILK.

WHERE DO POLAR BEARS VOTE?

THE NORTH POLL.

WHAT SOUND DO PORCUPINES MAKE WHEN THEY KISS?

OUCH!

WHY ARE FISH SO SMART?

BECAUSE THEY LIVE IN SCHOOLS.

WHY IS PIRATING SO ADDICTIVE?

THEY SAY ONCE YE LOSE YER FIRST HAND, YE GET HOOKED.

WHAT SONG DOES A CAT LIKE BEST?

THREE BLIND MICE.

WHY ARE CATS GOOD AT VIDEO GAMES?

BECAUSE THEY HAVE NINE LIVES.

WHAT IS A MONSTER'S FAVORITE DESSERT?

I SCREAM.

WHAT MONSTER PLAYS TRICKS ON HALLOWEEN?

PRANK-ENSTEIN.

HOW DOES A SNOWMAN LOSE WEIGHT?

HE WAITS FOR THE WEATHER TO GET WARMER.

WHAT KIND OF MUSIC DO MUMMIES LOVE?

WRAP MUSIC.

WHAT FRUIT DO SCARECROWS LOVE THE MOST?

STRAW-BERRIES.

WHAT KIND OF SHOES DO ROBBERS WEAR?

SNEAKERS.

WHAT DOES A WITCH USE TO DO HER HAIR?

SCARESPRAY.

WHAT IS A GHOST'S NOSE FULL OF?

BOO-GERS.

WHAT DO BIRDS SAY ON HALLOWEEN?

TRICK OR TWEET.

WHAT KIND OF PHOTOS DO ELVES TAKE?

ELFIES.

WHAT DO YOU CALL TWO WITCHES LIVING TOGETHER?

BROOMMATES.

WHAT INSTRUMENT DOES A SKELETON PLAY?

THE TROM-BONE.

WHO ISN'T HUNGRY AT THANKSGIVING?

THE TURKEY—HE'S ALREADY STUFFED.

WHY DID THE POLICE ARREST THE TURKEY?

THEY SUSPECTED IT OF FOWL PLAY.

WHAT DO ELVES LEARN IN SCHOOL?

THE ELF-ABET.

HOW DID THE SOGGY EASTER BUNNY DRY HIMSELF?

WITH A HARE DRYER.

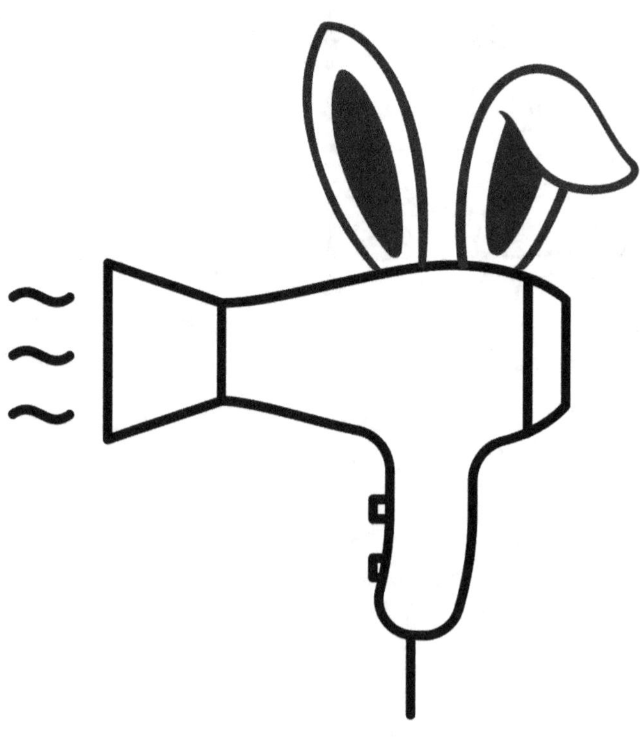

WHAT DO YOU CALL A REINDEER WITH BAD MANNERS?

RUDE-OLPH.

WHY ARE ELEVATOR JOKES SO GOOD?

THEY WORK ON MANY LEVELS.

WHAT DO ROAD CREWS USE AT THE NORTH POLE?

SNOW CONES.

WHAT HAPPENED WHEN THE EASTER BUNNY MET THE RABBIT OF HIS DREAMS?

THEY LIVED HOPPILY EVER AFTER.

WHY DID THE ROBBER JUMP IN THE SHOWER?

HE WANTED TO MAKE A CLEAN GETAWAY.

WHAT KIND OF NOISE DOES A WITCH'S VEHICLE MAKE?

BRRRROOOOM, BRRROOOOM.

WHAT DID TENNESSEE?

THE SAME THING AS ARKANSAS.

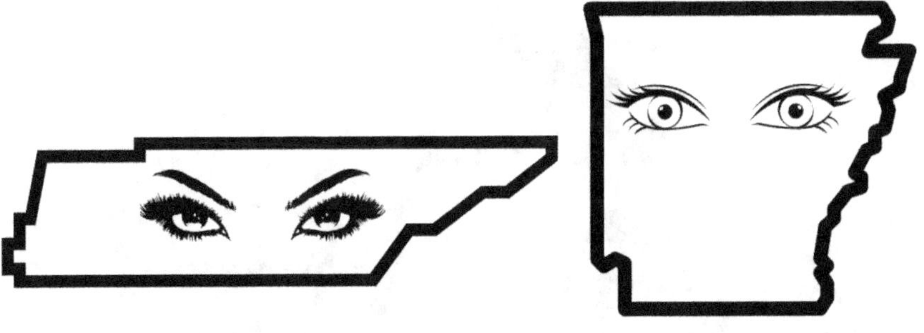

MY WIFE ASKED ME TO GO GET 6 CANS OF SPRITE FROM THE GROCERY STORE.

I REALIZED WHEN I GOT HOME THAT I HAD PICKED 7 UP.

WHY DO BEES HAVE STICKY HAIR?

BECAUSE THEY USE A HONEYCOMB.

DID YOU HEAR ABOUT THE KIDNAPPING AT SCHOOL?

IT'S FINE, HE WOKE UP.

WHY IS PETER PAN ALWAYS FLYING?

BECAUSE HE NEVERLANDS.

WHICH STATE HAS THE MOST STREETS?

RHODE ISLAND.

WHY DID THE COACH GO TO THE BANK?

TO GET HIS QUARTERBACK.

HOW DO CELEBRITIES STAY COOL?

THEY HAVE MANY FANS.

HOW DOES A PENGUIN BUILD HIS HOUSE?

IGLOOS IT TOGETHER.

WANT TO HEAR A JOKE ABOUT CONSTRUCTION?

I'M STILL WORKING ON IT.

FOR MORE HILARIOUS JOKES FOR KIDS, CHECK OUT THESE TITLES FROM SOLA PRINTING:

HILARIOUS SCHOOL JOKES

HILARIOUS DOG JOKES

HILARIOUS CAT JOKES

HILARIOUS ANIMAL JOKES

HILARIOUS FOOD JOKES

HILARIOUS SPORTS JOKES

HILARIOUS FARM JOKES

HILARIOUS SPACE JOKES

HILARIOUS CAMPING JOKES